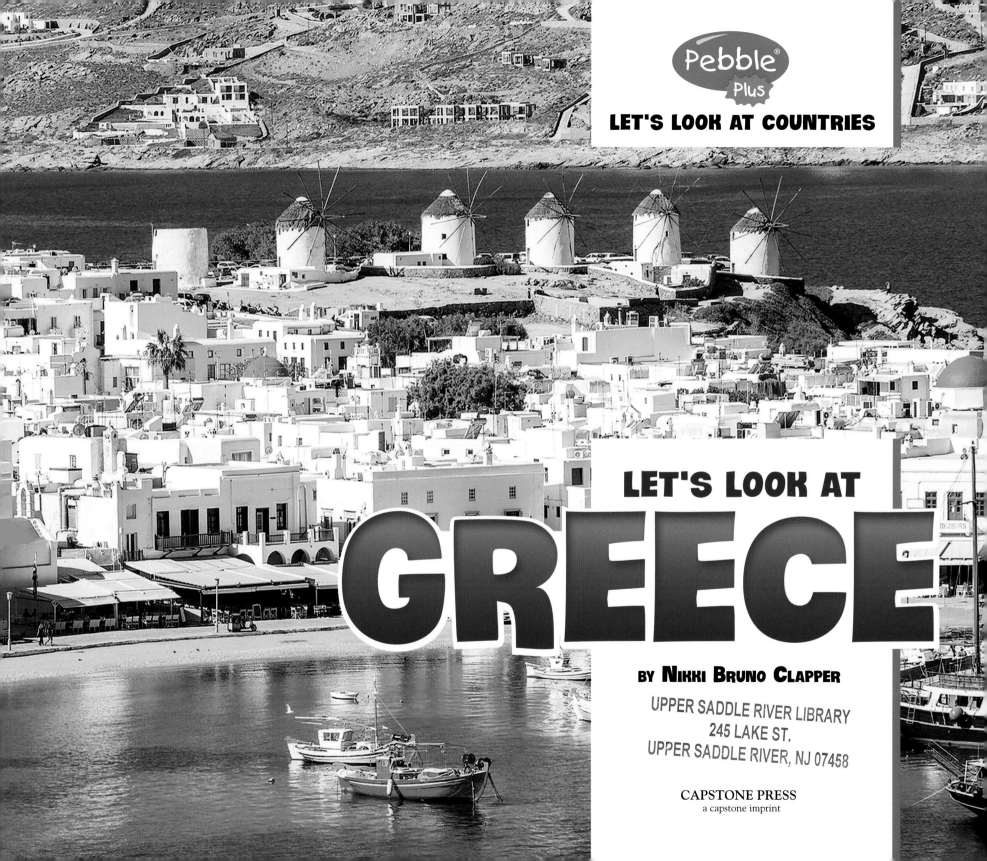

LET'S LOOK AT GREECE

BY NIKKI BRUNO CLAPPER

CAPSTONE PRESS
a capstone imprint

Pebble Plus is published by Capstone Press,
1710 Roe Crest Drive, North Mankato, Minnesota 56003
www.mycapstone.com

Library of Congress Cataloging-in-Publication Data
Names: Clapper, Nikki Bruno, author.
Title: Let's look at Greece / by Nikki Bruno Clapper.
Description: North Mankato, Minnesota : Capstone Press, [2018] | Series:
   Pebble plus. Let's look at countries | Includes bibliographical references
   and index. | Audience: Ages 4-8.
Identifiers: LCCN 2017037880 (print) | LCCN 2017038537 (ebook) | ISBN
   9781515799290 (eBook PDF) | ISBN 9781515799177 (hardcover) | ISBN
   9781515799238 (pbk.)
Subjects: LCSH: Greece--Juvenile literature.
Classification: LCC DF717 (ebook) | LCC DF717 .C53 2018 (print) | DDC
   949.5--dc23
LC record available at https://lccn.loc.gov/2017037880

Editorial Credits
Juliette Peters, designer; Tracy Cummins, media researcher; Laura Manthe, production specialist

Photo Credits
Getty Images: Jamie Squire, 17; Shutterstock: Antoine2K, 21, dinosmichail, 8-9, Evgeni Fabisuk,
11, franco lucato, 14-15, fritz16, Cover Top, Globe Turner, 22 Top, irakite, 10, Irma eyewink, 12-13,
Joshua Resnick, 18, Korpithas, 6-7, krivinis, Cover Bottom, Cover Back, Lev Paraskevopoulos, 5, Mila
Atkovska, 22-23, 24, nale, 4, Pawel Kazmierczak, 1, 19, Romas_Photo, Cover Middle, VOJTa Herout, 3

Note to Parents and Teachers

The Let's Look at Countries set supports national curriculum standards for social studies related to
people, places, and culture. This book describes and illustrates Greece. The images support early
readers in understanding the text. The repetition of words and phrases helps early readers learn
new words. This book also introduces early readers to subject-specific vocabulary words, which are
defined in the Glossary section. Early readers may need assistance to read some words and to use
the Table of Contents, Glossary, Read More, Internet Sites, Critical Thinking Questions, and Index
sections of the book.

Printed in the United States of America.
010774S18

TABLE OF CONTENTS

Where Is Greece?

Greece is a country in southern Europe. It is about the size of the U.S. state of Alabama. Greece's capital is Athens.

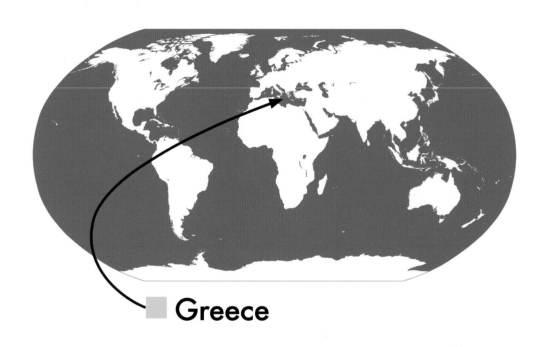

Greece

Islands and Mountains

Three seas circle

Greece's mainland.

More than 2,000 islands

dot the seas. Some beaches

have red or black sand.

Much of Greece's land
is rocky. Mountains cover
the mainland. Greece has
active volcanoes.

9

In the Wild

Wild goats climb

Greece's steep mountains.

Pelicans and other water

birds live on the coast.

Sea stars cling to rocks.

wild goats

pelican

People

People have lived in Greece
for 2,500 years. Many people
came from other parts
of Europe or from Asia.

On the Job

Many Greeks work in tourism. Others grow olives or catch fish for a living. Some families own small businesses.

olive picking

Olympic Birthplace

Sports are important

in Greece. The Olympic

Games started there.

Soccer and basketball

are favorite Greek sports.

At the Table

Greeks have a healthy diet.

They eat lots of seafood,

olives, and vegetables.

They snack on grape leaves.

Baklava is a sweet treat.

baklava

Famous Site

The Acropolis sits on a

hill in Athens. It has

many ancient temples.

Thousands of people

visit the Acropolis every day.

QUICK GREECE FACTS

Greek flag

Name: Hellenic Republic

Capital: Athens

Other major cities: Thessaloniki, Larisa, Patras

Population: 10,773,253 (July 2016 estimate)

Size: 50,949 square miles (131,957 sq km)

Language: Greek

Money: euro

GLOSSARY

active—currently erupting or likely to erupt

ancient—from a long time ago

baklava—a sweet treat made of dough and filled with nuts

capital—the city in a country where the government is based

mainland—the main part of a country that also has islands

temple—a building used for worship

tourism—the business of taking care of visitors to a country or place

volcano—an opening in the earth's surface that sometimes sends out hot lava, steam, and ash

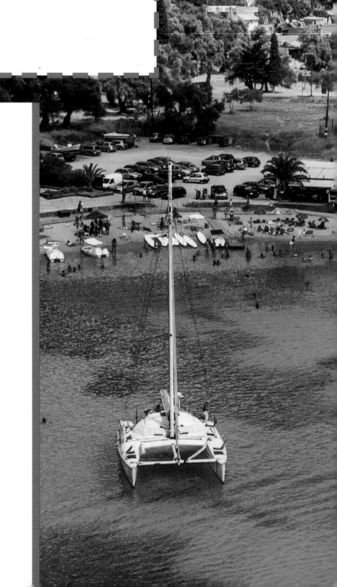

READ MORE

Murray, Julie. *Greece.* Explore the Countries. Minneapolis: ABDO Publishing Company, 2015.

Peppas, Lynn. *Cultural Traditions in Greece.* Cultural Traditions in My World. New York: Crabtree Pub., 2013.

Shoup, Kate. *Greece.* Exploring World Cultures. New York: Cavendish Square, 2017.

INTERNET SITES

Use FactHound to find Internet sites related to this book.

Visit *www.facthound.com*

Just type 9781515799177 and go.

Check out projects, games and lots more at
www.capstonekids.com

CRITICAL THINKING QUESTIONS

1. How do you think the mountains and volcanoes might affect how people live and travel on Greece's mainland?

2. Look at the photo on page 11. What features do pelicans have that might help them live near water?

3. What is a capital?

INDEX